GALE
CENGAGE Learning

Literary Newsmakers for Students, Volume 2

Project Editor
Anne Marie Hacht **Editorial**
Ira Mark Milne

Rights Acquisition and Management
Margaret Chamberlain-Gaston and Robyn Young
Manufacturing
Rita Wimberly

Imaging
Lezlie Light, Mike Logusz, and Kelly Quin
Product Design
Pamela A. E. Galbreath **Vendor Administration**
Civie Green **Product Manager**
Meggin Condino © 2006 Gale, a part of Cengage
Learning Inc.

For more information, contact
Gale, an imprint of Cengage Learning

agency, institution, publication, service, or individual does not imply endorsement of the editors or publisher. Errors brought to the attention of the publisher and verified to the satisfaction of the publisher will be corrected in future editions.

ISBN 13: 978-1-4144-0282-6
ISBN 10: 1-4144-0282-1
ISSN: 1559-9639

This title is also available as an e-book
ISBN-13: 978-1-4144-2930-4, ISBN-10: 1-4144-2930-4
Contact your Gale, an imprint of Cengage Learning representative for ordering information.

Printed in the United States of America

10 9 8 7 6 5 4 3 2 1

The Curious Incident of the Dog in the Night-Time

Mark Haddon

2003

Introduction

The Curious Incident of the Dog in the Night-time is Mark Haddon's first novel written for adults, though the book does appeal to a younger audience. The story is told through the perspective of an intelligent fifteen-year-old boy with autism who includes a variety of clever visuals to enhance his narrative. But Haddon says the novel is not simply about disability: "It's about what you can do with words and what it means to communicate with someone in a book." As noted by Dave Weich of Powells.com, Haddon never actually uses the word autism in the novel.

Christopher Boone narrates this novel after finding his neighbor's black poodle, Wellington, murdered with a garden fork. The book is Christopher's account of his investigation, and as he gets closer to the truth, he begins to investigate the personal mysteries in his family and discovers that the truths his father told him about his dead mother are indeed fiction.

Haddon's unique protagonist Christopher sees the world only in black and white, but through his ultra-rational and un-ironic prism, readers experience the spectrum of the boy's vibrant and vital mind. Many people suffering from autism and related disorders, as well as those who love and care for them, have celebrated the book as an enlightening peek into a mysterious world, though some have found fault with its presentation of the socially alienated. *The Curious Incident of the Dog in the Night-time* also has broad appeal to fiction fans around the world who enjoy the sincere, fresh, and funny whodunit. It is an international bestseller, which garnered a multitude of awards and landed on the prestigious list of Man Booker Prize nominees in 2003.

Author Biography

Born in Northampton, England, in 1962, Mark Haddon made a successful career out of writing children's books before publishing *The Curious Incident of the Dog in the Night-time*. In 1981, after receiving a bachelor's degree in English from Merton College, Oxford, Haddon held a variety of jobs, including several volunteer positions in which he helped people with physical and mental disabilities. A few years later, he returned to his studies to complete a master's degree in English Literature at Edinburgh University.

As a student at Edinburgh, he did illustrations for a number of magazines, and he has been a cartoonist for the *New Statesman, Spectator, Private Eye, Sunday Telegraph*, and *The Guardian*, where he co-wrote a cartoon strip, *Men—A User's Guide*.

In 1997, Haddon returned to England, where he won several awards for his involvement in a multitude of television projects, including two British Academy of Film and Television Arts (BAFTA) awards and The Royal Television Society Best Children's Drama for *Microsoap*. He also wrote two episodes for the children's TV series *Starstreet* and the BBC screenplay adaptation of Raymond Brigg's *Fungus and the Bogeyman*.

Mark Haddon penned over sixteen children's books before publishing his first novel for adults. *The Curious Incident of the Dog in the Night-time* has been published simultaneously in two imprints: David Frickling Books for young adult readers and the Jonathan Cape imprint for adults. The novel has sold co-editions in over fifteen countries and won both the Whitbread Book of the Year Award and a Commonwealth Writer's Award for Best First Book in 2003.

As of 2006, Haddon lives in Oxford with his wife and their son.

Plot Summary

Chapter 1: 2

The Curious Incident of the Dog in the Night-time begins with Christopher John Francis Boone finding Wellington, his next-door neighbor's black poodle, murdered. The dog is fatally stabbed with a garden fork and left on the lawn in front of Mrs. Shears's house. Christopher discovers the dog and wonders why someone wanted to kill him.

Chapter 2: 3

Christopher digresses from the murder to introduce himself to the reader. He also talks about how his teacher Siobhan showed him, through a series of smiley faces, the way to read other people's expressions and emotions. Sometimes Christopher cannot tell what pepole are thinking, even with Siobhan's helpful drawings. In that case, he simply walks away from them.

Chapter 3: 5

Christopher takes the reader back to the murder. He removes the fork from Wellington and holds the dog close. Mrs. Shears catches him in this compromising position and demands to know what he did to her dog. Christopher does not like her shouting and curls into a ball on the lawn to calm himself down.

Chapter 4: 7

Christopher again digresses, discussing the fact that this story is a "murder mystery novel." He describes the traits of a murder mystery novel and talks about how Siobhan told him to begin his story with an attention grabber. Christopher also mentions that he chose to write about Wellington's murder because he found the dog, and "some dogs were cleverer and more interesting than some people."

Chapter 5: 11

The police arrive on the scene to interrogate Christopher. Christopher hits one of the policemen when the policeman touches him. Christopher does not like being touched.

Chapter 6: 13

Christopher strays from the murder story to tell the reader "this will not be a funny book." He does not like jokes because he "do[es] not understand them."

Chapter 7: 17

Christopher is arrested. On the drive to the police station, he notices the stars and talks about the Big Bang Theory, as well as about how the end of the world will be marked by billions of falling stars. He offers a visual explaining how to view the most stars in our galaxy.

Chapter 8: 19

Christopher explains that he gave the chapters in his book prime numbers instead of regular numbers because he "like[s] prime numbers." He provides two small charts to illustrate how a person can find prime numbers.

Chapter 9: 23

At the police station, Christopher empties his pockets and describes the contents, but he becomes upset when the police try to take his watch. They let him keep the watch and ask him for a family contact. Though Christopher enjoys the small size of the cell, he imagines escaping.

Chapter 10: 29

Christopher thinks about how people are confusing to him because they do not say what they mean, particularly with regard to metaphors. To Christopher, metaphors resemble lies since they do not describe something precisely or truthfully.

Chapter 11: 31

Christopher's father, Ed Boone, arrives at the police station. Ed greets Christopher as they usually do: He spreads the fingers of his right hand spread out in a fan, Christopher does the same with his left, and they touch fingers and thumbs. Both Ed and the policeman ask Christopher about Wellington's murder. Christopher denies involvement, though he does say he meant to hit the policeman because the policeman touched him. Christopher is released from jail.

Chapter 12: 37

Christopher tells the reader why he does not tell lies. Since "there is ever only one thing which happened at a particular time and a particular place," there is only one truth.

Chapter 13: 41

On the way home from the police station, Christopher tells his father that he wants to discover who killed Wellington. Ed angrily tells Christopher to stop pursuing the case.

Chapter 14: 43

Christopher talks about the day his mother went to the hospital. Ed told him she went because of a problem with her heart and did not let him see her. Christopher decided to make a card for her, which his father promised to deliver the next day.

Chapter 15: 47

Christopher explains his "Good and Bad Day system": Seeing four red cars in a row means a day will be a Good Day; three red cars a Quite Good Day; five red cars a Super Good Day; and four yellow cars a Black Day, or a day when Christopher does not speak to anyone and "Take[s] No Risks." Mr. Jeavons, the school psychologist, calls Christopher "a very logical person" and a "very clever boy." Christopher also talks about his Uncle Terry, who thinks Christopher will not amount to much in the future, but Christopher comes to the logical conclusion that Terry is stupid. Christopher outlines his plans to attend university, where he will study mathematics or physics. Siobhan also offers to help him write his mystery story.

Chapter 16: 53

Christopher provides the reader with a visual of the get-well card he made for his mother. His father tells him that his mother died of a heart attack, but the news does not seem logical to Christopher. His mother "was very active" and "ate food which was healthy and high in fiber and low in saturated fat." Christopher asks what type of heart attack killed his mother, and his father does not know. Christopher supposes it was an aneurysm and discusses the term. Mrs. Shears comes to their house and makes dinner. She embraces Ed and plays Scrabble with Christopher.

Chapter 17: 59

Christopher decides to continue his investigation despite Ed's warning to stay out of other people's business. Christopher goes to Mrs. Shears and tells her that he wants to uncover the mystery of who killed her dog. Mrs. Shears balks and says goodbye. Christopher searches her garden shed and finds the garden fork that killed Wellington, but it is clean. Mrs. Shears orders him to leave her property and threatens to call the police.

Chapter 18: 61

In mentioning his mother's death, Christopher muses about heaven, God, death, and cremation. Once, Reverend Peters tried to explain the concepts of heaven and God, but Christopher does not follow the logic. He believes that when people die, "your brain stops working and your body rots." His mother was cremated and he imagines that since some of the smoke from the process went into the air, "molecules of Mother" were falling around the world.

Chapter 19: 67

Though Christopher has been taught not to talk to strangers, he decides to question the people who live along his street about what they saw with regard to the dog's murder. He speaks with Mr. Thompson in number 40, and avoids the neighbors who take drugs in number 38. Mr. Wise and his mother in number 43 are not home. Mrs. Alexander in number 39 invites him inside for biscuits and orange squash juice. When he does not want to go inside with her, she offers to bring the treats outside. He leaves before she can return because he is not sure what she is doing in her house to prepare the treats. Christopher suspects Mr. Shears of the murder and provides a "Chain of Reasoning" for the reader.

Chapter 20: 71

Christopher talks about the special-needs students at his school. He believes the term "special needs" is stupid because every person has special needs. He mentions Siobhan as an example, and how she must wear glasses to see. He discusses taking his A-levels in math and tells the story of how Mrs. Gascoyne, the head mistress, did not want him to take the exam. His father argued with her until she gave in. Christopher plans to acquire his degree in math or physics, then "get a job and earn lots of money."

Chapter 21: 73

Christopher recalls a time when he believed his behavior would cause his parents to divorce, particularly because they would shout about it. He provides a list of his behavioral problems for the reader.

Chapter 22: 79

Mrs. Shears calls Ed Boone about Christopher

being in her garden. Christopher tells his father he was doing detective work to find out who killed Wellington. He informs his father that Mr. Shears is the primary suspect. Ed becomes furious and wants Christopher to stop investigating the incident. He makes Christopher promise "to give up this ridiculous game."

Chapter 23: 83

Christopher gives reasons why he would be a good astronaut. He enjoys being in small spaces, would not miss home, and could use his pet rat Toby in experiments. In addition, he would not have to socialize with people, except through transmissions from Mission Control.

Chapter 24: 89

Christopher tells Siobhan that his father does not want him to investigate Wellington's murder any further. After reading his book, Siobhan praises his work thus far, but Christopher is not satisfied because he did not solve the murder. Siobhan tries to help Christopher figure out why his father wants him to stop trying to solve the mystery. Christopher has two Black Days in a row.

Chapter 25: 97

On a Super Good Day, Christopher believes something special will happen. Christopher rationalizes what his father made him promise and, when he encounters Mrs. Alexander at the grocery, asks her questions about Mr. Shears. Mrs. Alexander tells him that his mother was "good friends" with Mr. Shears, and Christopher deduces that they "did sex" with each other.

Chapter 26: 101

Christopher talks about why he likes numbers. He illustrates the "Monty Hall problem," which he read about in the *Parade* magazine's "Ask Marilyn" column. The problem shows numbers can be complicated, but logical. Logical reasoning brings answers.

Chapter 27: 103

Ed Boone's employee Rhodri is at Christopher's house when he returns home from the grocery. His father asks where he was since he is a bit late. Christopher tells him a white lie. Rhodri gives him a mathematical equation to solve. Christopher thinks about adding more description to his mystery novel, per Siobhan's advice.

Chapter 28: 107

Christopher summarizes his favorite book, *The Hound of the Baskervilles*. He critiques the bits he likes and does not like. He also lists the clues and red herrings in the novel and compares Sherlock to himself. Sherlock "doesn't believe in the supernatural, which is God and fairy tales and

Hounds of Hell and curses, which are stupid things."

Chapter 29: 109

After Christopher shows Siobhan more of the book he is writing, she asks him if learning about his mother made him sad. He says no, because feeling sad is stupid, or illogical. He also shows the reader a picture of an alien he drew in art class with Mrs. Peters.

Chapter 30: 113

Christopher describes his memory in terms of a film. He can "rewind" to particular distinct memories and can recognize people by searching through his mind to see if he met them before. He compares those pictures in his head that are made from real memories to those pictures that are not to figure out how to handle different situations.

Chapter 31: 127

When Christopher comes home from school, he leaves his belongings on the kitchen table, including the mystery book he is writing. While Christopher watches a *Blue Planet* video, his father arrives home from work and finds the book. Ed Boone becomes furious at Christopher for continuing to investigate the mystery. He grabs Christopher in anger, and because Christopher does not like being touched, they get into a physical fight that Christopher does not completely remember. Ed takes Christopher's book.

Chapter 32: 131

Christopher provides a list of the reasons why he does not like yellow or brown. He also explains why having likes and dislikes is not silly.

Chapter 33: 137

As an apology for their fight, Ed takes Christopher to the Twycross Zoo. Christopher lists his favorite animals and provides a map of the zoo. Ed tells Christopher that he loves him and that he does not want Christopher to get hurt. Christopher does not quite understand.

Chapter 34: 139

Christopher talks about how he likes Sherlock Holmes but not Sir Arthur Conan Doyle. Doyle was spiritual, which is not logical. Doyle said in an article that he believed in the Cottingley Fairies, which were obviously fake.

Chapter 35: 149

Siobhan asks Christopher about the bruise on his face. When Christopher tells her that his father hurt him, she questions him to make sure he is all right. After school Christopher searches the house for his book and finally finds it in his father's clothes cupboard. Christopher also finds a bunch of envelopes addressed to him. When he hears his father come home from work, he takes an envelope and hides it under his mattress. Later when he is alone, he opens the envelope and finds a letter from his mother. She says it has been a while since her last letter because she got a new job as a secretary in a steel factory and moved into a new flat. Christopher is confused. He wonders how it could be from his mother and decides to solve that mystery too. He plans to look at the other letters in his father's cupboard.

Chapter 36: 151

Christopher explains that science will eventually unlock most mysteries and explain phenomena such as ghosts. He uses a variety of charts to explain the fluctuations in the frog population in the pond at his school.

Chapter 37: 157

Six days later, when Ed Boone works late, Christopher returns to the forty-three letters in his father's cupboard and begins to read them. The letters express his mother's love for Christopher as she tells him about her new home, her new jobs, and her memories of him. She regrets not being a good mother and explains that she left because she could not raise Christopher with the kind of patience he needed. Roger Shears was the only person she could confide in about her inadequacies. She had intended to say goodbye to Christopher but his father had not let her. After Christopher reads four letters, he realizes that his mother did not die as his father said. Ed lied to him. Christopher becomes sick at the notion, vomits, and loses track of time. His father finds him and tries to explain while helping to clean Christopher up.

Chapter 38: 163

Christopher explains how people's minds work like computers, "not because they are special but because they have to keep turning off for fractions of a second while the screen changes" and "people always think there is something special about what they can't see."

Chapter 39: 167

Ed continues to explain his actions, and in doing so, admits to killing Wellington. He tells Christopher how Mrs. Shears helped him deal with Christopher's mom leaving, but Mrs. Shears liked her independence and her dog better than she liked him. Christopher becomes frightened by the truth. He can no longer trust his father because his father told a big lie. He is afraid his father might try to kill him. Christopher takes Toby, puts on his coat, retrieves his special food box, and hides in their shed.

Chapter 40: 173

Christopher discusses the truth of stars and how there is not really magic in constellations.

Chapter 41: 179

Christopher spends the night in the shed. He looks to the sky and stars to keep him calm and his mind busy. His father searches for him but does not find him. Christopher thinks about living with Mrs. Shears because she is not a stranger, but Mrs. Shears is not home when he tries knocking on her door. He thinks about staying with Mrs. Alexander, but rules that possibility out because she is a stranger. After much deliberation and two charts, he decides to live with his mother in London.

Christopher is in emotional distress. He tries dealing with it by formulating a plan. He asks Mrs. Alexander to look after Toby. Mrs. Alexander coaxes him to talk everything over with her, but Christopher leaves. He goes to school to ask Siobhan where the train is, but he sees his father's truck parked in front. Afraid and anxious, he gets sick and realizes he will have to ask a stranger for directions. He asks a woman with a little boy where he might buy a map because "ladies are safer." When she learns where he wants to go, she points him toward the train station. Christopher becomes frightened and confused on the way, but he finally finds the station by moving in a spiral path. He provides the reader with a map.

Chapter 42: 181

Christopher provides two lists and a drawing of a cow to illustrate how he notices everything about the world around him. Sometimes he notices too many things at once and it affects his brain like a computer crashing. He has to shut down and reboot. He also clarifies the fact that he does know a few jokes, and he tells one about an economist, a logician, and a mathematician.

Chapter 43: 191

Christopher maps out the train station. He is afraid and confused by the commotion, but he does a math problem, which he illustrates, to clear his head. A policeman questions him about who he is and where he is going. Christopher tells him he will live with his mother. The policeman helps Christopher retrieve money from an ATM and buy a train ticket. Christopher boards a train to London.

Chapter 44: 193

Christopher compares his personal timetable (the timetable he used after his mother left) to a train's schedule. He likes timetables because he likes to know when everything will happen. He considers his timetable "a map of time" that shows "the relationship between the way different things change." He also offers "a map of everything and everywhere" and explains how "time is a mystery." Timetables keep him from getting tangled in the mystery.

Chapter 45: 197

The policeman catches Christopher on the train and tells him that Ed Boone is at the police station waiting for him back in Swindon. Christopher tells the cop that he is going to London to live with his mother and that his father should be arrested for killing Wellington. Christopher screams when the cop tries to touch him. The policeman calls the station and says he will get off at the next stop and bring Christopher with him. Christopher becomes overwhelmed looking out the window and tries to clear his head with a math problem. During the ride, he needs to use the bathroom, which he does not like because it smells like the toilet at his school. He uses the toilet despite his discomfort, and then decides to curl up on a luggage rack where he does more math to keep himself occupied. The policeman hunts for him but does not find him.

Chapter 46: 199

Christopher ruminates on why people believe in God and why there is life on Earth: "the world is very complicated" and nothing "could happen by chance." Christopher thinks people should think logically about the subject and see that life "just happens."

Chapter 47: 211

Christopher remains in his hiding place even though he encounters a few passengers collecting their luggage. When he finally leaves the spot and returns to his seat, he discovers his belongings are gone, along with the policeman. Christopher gets off the train, and he becomes overwhelmed by the noise and confusion of the station. He goes to an information booth and asks how to get to his mother's house. When he provides the address, the lady directs him toward the subway. Though he is frightened, he watches the activity in the station and figures out how to use an escalator, buy a ticket, and find the correct subway line. Once in the correct station, however, Christopher is sickened by the crowded windowless Underground and sits on a bench while waiting for the feeling to pass. He desperately wishes he were home.

Chapter 48: 223

While waiting to get better, Christopher offers the reader a description and a drawing of the advertisement on the wall of the Underground station. He also talks about the meaning of holidays, orangutans, and advertisements.

Chapter 49: 227

After calming himself down, Christopher realizes Toby has run away from his pocket. He decides to look for Toby because the station is no longer crowded. He sees the rat down by the rails and goes to catch him. As a train approaches, a man "with diamond patterns on his socks" warns Christopher and tries to grab him, but Christopher screams. Toby bites Christopher, but Christopher holds tight to the rat with both hands as the train bears down. The man with the strange socks pulls Christopher up from the rails, but Christopher screams at the physical contact. They both fall onto the platform, and though they are safe from the train, Christopher hurts his shoulder and the man scrapes his face. Christopher runs to the bench with Toby, and the man yells at him for his careless actions. A lady approaches to ask if he is all right and tries to touch him, but Christopher screams again. Frightened, he threatens to cut her with his Swiss Army knife. The man and woman leave, remarking on his crazy behavior.

Christopher finally gets on the train to Willesden Junction. Though he does not like the number of people on the train (eleven), he focuses on his surroundings to ease his mind. He illustrates the pattern on the seats and times the arrival at each coming station. He gets off at Willesden Junction and after some deliberation, goes into a little shop and buys a map in a book form, which he likes. He shows the maps of Willesden Junction and his route to get there. He follows his route to his mother's address and reports that "the only interesting thing that happened on the way was 8 men dressed up in Viking costumes with helmets with horns on and they were shouting" and that "he had to go for another wee" and "went in the alleyway." No one answers at his mother's house so he waits by the dustbins until his mother finally arrives. When she sees him, she tries hugging him but he pushes her away. He knocks himself over with the force of the shove. Toby escapes, and though his mother remembers to greet him with a hand gesture, Christopher focuses on catching his rat. His mother asks how he got there and Christopher recounts the story briefly. He also tells his mother that his father killed Wellington and he came to live with her.

Once inside the flat, Christopher makes a map of the house, which he provides in the book. During a bath, Christopher's mother asks him why he never answered her letters. Christopher tells her he thought she was dead and explains how he found the letters. His mother is furious at the news. She asks to hold Christopher's hand, but he tells her he does not like anyone holding his hand. A policeman shows up at the flat to ask Christopher some questions about why he ran away. His mother says he can live with her. In the middle of the night, Christopher awakens to shouting. He hears his father arguing with his mother and Mr. Shears, who lives with his mother. They fight about the lie Ed Boone told about the mother's death and about the mother leaving. Christopher's father tries to talk to him, but Christopher is frightened. After Mr. Shears calls the police, the policeman returns to take Christopher's father away.

Chapter 50: 229

Christopher has his favorite dream: that everyone in the world dies from a virus which is caused by the expressions on people's faces and the only ones left are people like him. He can travel anywhere without fear of being touched or addressed, and he can go anywhere he wants and do anything he wants.

Chapter 51: 233

Mr. Shears does not want Christopher to stay with them for more than a few days. Christopher's mother takes the day off so she and Christopher can buy some supplies for his stay. Christopher becomes upset when the store is too crowded and they return home in a taxi. Christopher's mother leaves him home and goes back to the store where she buys him a pair of pajamas with a star-pattern, which Christopher illustrates. He tells his mother he must go back to Swindon and take his A-level examination in math. His mother says that will not be possible. That night, Christopher takes a walk in the neighborhood when he cannot sleep and hides in a small place. When his mother calls for him, he emerges from the hiding spot, and she tells him not to run off again. The next day while his mother goes shopping, he watches *Star Trek* videos, and the following day, his mother is fired from her job because she has missed too many days helping Christopher settle in. Christopher reminds his mother he has to return to Swindon to take his A-levels. His mother becomes angry and tells him he must postpone the exam. She feels pressured by his father, who wants to take her to court, and Mr. Shears, who wants no part of the situation. Christopher feels anxious about not taking his A-levels, but his Good Day system does not work in this neighborhood, which makes him feel worse.

To make it up to Christopher, his mother takes him to a hill where they watch airplanes from Heathrow Airport and eat ice cream. His mother tells him that she talked to Mrs. Gascoyne and Christopher will take his A-levels next year. Christopher becomes upset. His mother tries to soothe him with science books and a food chart. Mr. Shears comes into Christopher's bedroom after drinking and threatens Christopher. The next morning, Christopher's mother packs their belongings into Mr. Shears's car, and they drive to Swindon. Christopher hopes he will get to do his A-levels. Ed Boone is surprised to see them in his flat, and while he argues with Christopher's mother, Christopher tries to drown out the noise by playing the bongo drums given to him by his Uncle Terry. Later, when things calm down, Christopher asks his mother if he can do his A-levels, and his mother tells him again that he will have to wait until next year.

When Christopher and his mother get in the car to go to school the next day, Mrs. Shears confronts his mother, and they briefly argue. At school, Siobhan meets Christopher's mother. When his mother leaves, Siobhan says there is a chance he can still do his A-levels if he wants. Reverend Peters acts as the invigilator, or supervisor, as originally planned. Because of the upsetting events of the previous few days, Christopher finds himself anxious during the exam, but he eventually settles down to work the problems. Back at home,

Christopher still does not like being alone with his father. Mr. Shears arrives at the house in a taxi and dumps a box of Christopher's mother's belongings on the lawn. Ed Boone asks Christopher how his exam went, and his mother coaxes him to answer. His father appreciates the brief moment of Christopher's attention. His father tells his mother that she has to move out of the house, and she finds a small apartment and a job. Christopher asks if his father will be arrested for murdering the dog, and his mother says it depends if Mrs. Shears presses charges. Christopher's mother's new apartment is small and does not have its own bathroom. Christopher does not like sharing a bathroom with other people. His mother buys him a puzzle, which he illustrates.

Christopher has to stay at his father's house after school until his mother comes home from work. He does not like staying with his father and locks the bedroom door. Toby dies. One day, Christopher's father asks if he can talk with him. He tells Christopher that he wants Christopher to learn how to trust him again. He brings Christopher a dog. Christopher cannot take the dog to his mother's house because the house is too small. Christopher receives an A on his A-level exam. He feels happy and shows this with a smiley face. He names the dog Sandy, and when his mother gets the flu, he stays with his father for three days. He helps his father make a vegetable garden, buys a preparation guide for taking future A-level exams, and reminds the reader that he will "go to university … live in a flat with a proper garden … and become a scientist."

Appendix

Christopher illustrates his favorite math problem from the A-level exam.

Characters

Alexander

Mrs. Alexander lives at Number 39 Randolph Street. Christopher first meets her as she is trimming her front hedge. She invites Christopher over for biscuits and tea, but he leaves before she can return with the treats because he does not know her well enough and becomes nervous. Christopher meets Mrs. Alexander for the second time at the grocery at the end of his street. He asks her questions to further investigate Wellington's murder. She tells Christopher about his mother's relationship with Mr. Shears. When Christopher leaves town, he asks Mrs. Alexander to take care of Toby, but he ends up taking the rat with him. Mrs. Alexander has a dachshund named Ivor.

Christopher John Francis Boone

Fifteen-year-old Christopher narrates *The Curious Incident of the Dog in the Night-time* from a first-person point of view. Christopher is autistic, logical, and highly intelligent, and he decides to solve the murder of Wellington, the dog owned by Mrs. Shears, his next-door neighbor. Christopher only likes people who tell the truth. He knows all the world capitals and every prime number up to 7,057. His dislike for the colors yellow and brown sometimes sours his mood. He is interested in astronomy and believes he would make a good astronaut because he likes small, dark places. He enjoys math, mysteries, and maps and uses the skills needed for all three to solve the murder of Wellington. He groans when provided with too much information at once. In the future, he wants to attend university and study physics or mathematics. At the start of the novel, he has a pet rat, Toby. At the novel's close, his father gets him a dog, Sandy.

Media Adaptations

- *The Curious Incident of the Dog in the Night-time* was released as an unabridged audiobook by Recorded Books in 2003. It is narrated by Jeff Woodman.

- *The Curious Incident of the Dog in the Night-time* was released as an abridged audiobook by Random House in 2004. It is narrated by Ben

Tibber and available as a CD or audiocassette.

Ed Boone

Ed is Christopher's father. He runs a heating maintenance and boiler repair business with his employee, Rhodri. Ed serves as Christopher's primary caregiver after Christopher's mother leaves the family. To protect Christopher, Ed lies, telling him that she died from a heart attack. In addition, Ed hides the letters Christopher's mother sends to Christopher under his bed. After Christopher's mother left, Ed had an affair with Eileen Shears and, when Eileen did not completely reciprocate his feelings, Ed accidentally killed her dog, Wellington. Ed does want the best for Christopher and encourages him to take his A-level examinations. He buys Christopher a dog, Sandy, to help make up for the lies he told.

Terry Boone

Uncle Terry is Ed Boone's brother. Terry calls Christopher a "spazzer," but Christopher believes it is a proven fact that Terry is stupid. Terry has a tattoo on his arm, and according to Christopher, would probably never attend college. Terry works in a bread factory.

Christopher's Mother

Christopher's father, Ed, tells Christopher that his mother died from a heart attack, but in reality, she had an affair with their neighbor, Roger Shears, and moved to London. Raising Christopher was too hard for her to bear; she did not have the patience necessary to deal with his autism. She sent letters to Christopher, which Ed kept hidden beneath his bed. Christopher remembered his mother as a "small person who smelled nice" and "wore a fleece with a zip down the front." She was thirty-eight years old when she divorced Ed Boone and left Christopher. According to Christopher, she "rode a bicycle and ate food which was healthy and high in fiber." After moving to London, she worked as a secretary in a steel factory and then for a "Chartered Surveyors" office.

Gascoyne

Mrs. Gascoyne is the headmistress at Christopher's school. Ed Boone struggles to convince her to let Christopher take his A-level exams.

Jeavons

The psychologist at Christopher's school, Mr. Jeavons asks Christopher about his peculiarities, habits, and personal thoughts. He considers Christopher "a very logical person" and a "very clever boy." He "smells of soap and wears brown shoes with approximately sixty tiny circular holes in each of them." Mr. Jeavons understands why

Christopher enjoys math, but Christopher does not think Mr. Jeavons knows anything about the subject.

Peters

Reverend Peters comes to Christopher's school from time to time to talk about religion. Christopher asks him about heaven and God, but Reverend Peters brushes Christopher off. Reverend Peters is the invigilator for Christopher's A-level examination. He smokes during the exam and reads *The Cost of Discipleship* by Dietrich Bonhoeffer.

Rhodri

Rhodri works with Ed Boone in Ed's heating maintenance and boiler repair business. He is friendly to Christopher and gives him math problems to solve. Christopher does not like it when Rhodri laughs at him. Sometimes he drinks beer after work with Ed Boone.

Eileen Shears

Eileen Shears had an affair with Ed Boone after Ed's wife ran off with her husband, Roger. Eileen lives next door and is the owner of Wellington, the murdered dog. Though she took care of Ed and Christopher when Ed's wife left, Eileen prefers her independence and her life with Wellington over a permanent relationship with Ed.

Roger Shears

Roger, the Boones' former neighbor, had an affair with Ed's wife. They ran away together to London where Roger works for a bank. Roger has a quick temper and does not want Christopher to stay too long when he arrives in London to find his mother.

Siobhan

Siobhan is a teacher at Christopher's school and also his good friend, though Christopher does not classify her as such. She advises him to write a book that begins with an attention grabber. She has "long blond hair and wears glasses which are made of green plastic." She teaches Christopher about rhetorical questions, holidays, and how to read expressions on people's faces.

Wellington

Wellington is the dog that Christopher finds murdered. Wellington was a "big poodle" with "curly black fur." Christopher is determined to discover who fatally stabbed him with a garden fork.

Themes

Truth

Throughout the novel, Christopher Boone emphasizes his inability to tell anything but the truth. "I do not tell lies," he says in Chapter 12:37. "I can't tell lies." The conflict in the book comes from Christopher's desperate attempt to make sense of his father's lies. After Christopher finds letters from his mother in his father's bedroom cupboard, he realizes his father did not tell him the truth about his mother's supposed heart attack. As his father tries to explain that he was only protecting Christopher, another lie is revealed: Christopher's father killed Wellington the dog. Christopher cannot process lies, because he believes that there was "only ever one thing which happened at a particular time and a particular place."

Attention to Detail

Although autism causes Christopher Boone to meticulously note every detail of the world around him with fervent need, the careful attention prompts the reader to examine his own surroundings more closely. Christopher's keen eye and precise plans may appear obsessive-compulsive, yet they teach the reader an important and positive lesson in how to interact with other people, how to experience new places, and how to approach new situations.

Certainly not every cow in a field must be counted, but Christopher's reasoning reminds the reader that even those people who are not adventurous and often stay inside their comfort zone have nothing to fear if they plan accordingly and proceed one step at a time. When Christopher becomes overwhelmed by sensory overload at times, he calms himself by solving mathematical equations, counting cows, or looking at the stars. This self-comfort prompts the reader to imagine personal ways that one might handle stressful situations. Even Christopher retreating to a bench at the subway station shows it is possible to manage overwhelming anxiety.

The Order of Life

In an interview for Powells.com, Haddon says,

> All of us feel, to a certain extent, alienated from the stuff going on around us. And all of us at some point, rather like Christopher, have chaos entering our lives. We have these limited strategies we desperately use to try to put our lives back in order.

The Curious Incident of the Dog in the Night-time focuses on Christopher Boone's need to put together pieces of this mystery. He uses his deductive reasoning skills and his keen eye for detail to find the truth, in terms of uncovering both Wellington's killer and his father's secrets. Only when the world encroaches on his personal space or overwhelms him does Christopher lose control.

Style

First-Person Point of View

The Curious Incident of the Dog in the Night-time is written from the first-person point of view. Christopher Boone writes his personal account of a mystery, the murder of Wellington the dog, and along the way, becomes involved in the mystery of his mother's death. Christopher's first-person account is credible and detailed. Perhaps Christopher's autistic condition allows the reader to easily believe him when he claims that he cannot tell lies. In any case, the vast amount of straight-forward, deductive detail that Christopher provides coaxes the reader into believing his tale.

Structure

Prime numbers make up the most superficial structural element of *The Curious Incident of the Dog in the Night-time*. Because Christopher Boone likes prime numbers, he uses them to order the chapters, rather than cardinal numbers. Prime numbers also reflect the mystery narrative in the novel. In Christopher's opinion, figuring out which numbers are prime is rather like solving a mystery because they "are what is left when you have taken all the patterns away."

Two mystery narratives frame the story: the

murder of Wellington and the secret of Christopher's mother's "death." Just as Christopher details the world to move comfortably through it, he must pay attention to the events of each mystery to solve it. The book follows Christopher's process step by step, clue by clue, until the narratives culminate in the truth near the end of the novel. Among the chapters that push the mysteries closer to revelation, Christopher digresses, filling other chapters with personal thoughts on life, God, stars, and white lies.

Motifs

Throughout the novel, plans, maps, drawings, and other visuals illustrate Christopher's need to physically and mentally record the world and his actions within it. Just as Christopher enjoys timetables because they note "when everything is going to happen," lists and pictures help Christopher remember how to predict and deal with certain situations and things.

Christopher Boone leans on numbers as a logical means to make sense out of the world. When situations, settings, and people confuse or upset him, he turns to mathematical equations to calm himself. Mathematics also represent the future for Christopher; he hopes to pass his A-levels, then go to university where he will study either mathematics or physics and make a new independent life for himself. Numbers also help Christopher keep track of his behavioral problems, his likes and dislikes, and his daily activities.

Topics for Further Study

- Christopher Boone notices every detail of the world around him. Though Christopher's autism inspires his attentiveness, every reader can learn from his approach to life. Using Christopher's keen senses as inspiration, write an essay describing your bedroom, your classroom, or your favorite place to a friend.

- Throughout *The Curious Incident of the Dog in the Night-time*, Christopher learns how to define and tell white lies. Early in the story, he says he "is a good person" because he "can't tell lies." Christopher defines a white lie as "not a lie at all," but "where you tell the truth but you do not tell all of the truth." Discuss the difference between white lies and regular lies with a friend or small group. Afterward, write an essay that summarizes your thoughts regarding white lies and regular lies. Include a personal experience to illustrate your thoughts.

- The entire novel is written from Christopher's point of view. Think about how this story would be different if it included Siobhan's, Ed Boone's, or even Mrs. Alexander's point of view. Write an essay answering one or more of the following questions: How would having the point of view of other characters in the novel alter the story's credibility? How would having their point of view change a reader's perception of Christopher? How would a different narrative style modify the mystery elements?

- *The Curious Incident of the Dog in the Night-time* is an unusual novel for many of reasons. One obvious difference between this novel and others is Mark Haddon's use of visuals, rather than just text. Write an essay about at least three visual cues in the novel. Discuss how they add an additional dimension to the characterization of Christopher as well as to the development of the plot.

- Do you think that the term "love" applies to the relationship between Christopher and his parents? Between Christopher's mother and Mr. Shears? Is Christopher capable of love as you define it? Divide into pairs and examine these questions by taking turns adopting the perspectives of the pairs of characters in the novel who are arguably joined by love: Christopher and his father, Christopher and his mother, Christopher's mother and Mr. Shears, Christopher's father and Mrs. Shears.

Autism

Autism is a brain disorder usually diagnosed in children younger than three. Like Christopher Boone, people with autism typically have problems with social interaction and communication, and changes in routine can often be upsetting for them. Repetitive preoccupations and an obsessive interest in languages, numbers, and symbols also characterize a person with autism. At this time, the cause of autism is unknown, though many experts believe it to be a genetic-based disorder that occurs before birth.

Christopher Boone has a particular form of autism called Asperger's Syndrome, or A. S. His obsession with detail, mathematics, colors, and astronomy, as well as his unwavering attention to routine and violent aversion to socialization, all reflect his condition, though it is unnamed in the novel.

Asperger Syndrome is a form of autism first noticed in 1944 by Hans Asperger, a German doctor. According to Barbara L. Kirby, founder of *Online Asperger Syndrome Information and Support* and co-author of *The Oasis Guide to Asperger Syndrome*:

[People with A. S.] have a great deal

of difficulty reading nonverbal cues (body language) and very often the individual with AS has difficulty determining proper body space. Often overly sensitive to sounds, tastes, smells, and sights, the person with AS may prefer soft clothing, certain foods, and be bothered by sounds or lights no one else seems to hear or see.

The National Institute of Neurological Disorders and Stroke explains:

Children with A. S. want to know everything about their topic of interest and their conversations with others will be about little else. Their expertise, high level of vocabulary, and formal speech patterns make them seem like little professors. Other characteristics of A. S. include repetitive routines or rituals; peculiarities in speech and language; socially and emotionally inappropriate behavior and the inability to interact successfully with peers; problems with nonverbal communication; and clumsy and uncoordinated motor movements.

Math-related Jobs

In *The Curious Incident of the Dog in Night-*

time, Christopher Boone imagines a future career in mathematics or physics. As Christopher demonstrates in the novel, studying mathematics requires patience, attention to detail, discipline, and keen problem-solving skills. The career office at the Massachusetts Institute of Technology lists medicine, government, education, environment, scientific writing, and information science as possible fields for students like Christopher who are interested in mathematics as a career choice. People skilled in math can work as computer programmers, accountants, financiers, systems analysts, medical researchers, auditors, cryptographers, teachers, and software designers, to name just a few occupations. A civil engineer, for example, uses math to plan and design transport systems or to analyze construction materials. Comparably, a research scientist might need math to study automobile emissions and alternative fuels.

Poodles

Christopher Boone's mysterious adventure begins when the dog Wellington, "Not one of the small poodles that have hairstyles but a big poodle," is murdered. The American Kennel Club describes the breed: "Carrying himself proudly, very active, intelligent, the Poodle has about him an air of distinction and dignity peculiar to himself." Thus, Mark Haddon's choice for a murdered dog quite symbolic and extremely relative to the novel's exceptional protagonist, Christopher Boone.

While Wellington may not have had a hairstyle, Christopher is wrong that "big" (standard) poodles do not have hairstyles. The poodle was bred as a water dog, retrieving its master's quarry from cold waters. Its distinctive cuts originated from a practical purpose: to streamline the dog for swimming while protecting its vulnerable joints and organs from the cold. The poodle comes in three sizes: The standard is over fifteen inches in height at the shoulder; the miniature is between ten and fifteen inches tall; and the toy is smaller than ten inches. The range of sizes available in a dog that is calm, intelligent, and less apt to shed than a straight-haired dog have made the poodle a very popular pet.

Critical Overview

Although many readers shy away from books about people with disabilities, *The Curious Incident of the Dog in the Night-time* inspires the public to take a chance on Christopher Boone, a fifteen-year-old boy with autism who narrates the novel. As Jackie Gropman from the *School Library Journal* explained, "his story evokes emotions in readers—heartache and frustration for his well-meaning but clueless parents and deep empathy for the wonderfully honest, funny, and lovable protagonist. Readers will never view the behavior of an autistic person again without more compassion and understanding."

Said Mel Gussow of the *New York Times*, "Mr. Haddon performed the literary equivalent of a hat trick in hockey, scoring three goals with one book: high critical praise and the admiration of other novelists, from Ian McEwan to Anne Tyler; soaring sales; and wide readership by both adults and children." Gussow also noted, "the book is layered with mystery and deadpan comedy. It also offers a deeply sensitive portrait of one of the most unusual adolescents one is likely to meet in or out of fiction." On the publisher's website, Arthur Golden, author of the best-selling novel *Memoirs of a Geisha* is quoted as saying, "I have never read anything quite like Mark Haddon's funny and agonizingly honest book, or encountered a narrator more vivid and memorable."

The Curious Incident of the Dog in the Night-time won Britain's 2004 Whitbread Book of the Year Award. The novel won a 2003 Listen Up Award, a 2004 Alex Award, and a 2006 British Book Award.

What Do I Read Next?

- *A Spot of Bother* (2006) is Mark Haddon's second novel for adults and another humorous tale of an unlikely hero trying to navigate the perils of family and social relationships.

- *Forrest Gump* (2002), by Winston Groom, is a story about an "idiot savant" that spans forty years of history and turns a simple man's life into an epic. The novel, like *The Curious Incident of the Dog in the Night-time*, is written in first-person.

- In *Hurricane Dancing: Glimpses of Life with an Autistic Child* (2004), poet D. Alison Watt and photographer Carole Ruth Fields reveal the emotional experiences of raising an autistic child through a striking combination of photographs and poetry.

- Virginia Woolf's post-World War I novel *Mrs. Dalloway* follows Clarissa Dalloway through London on the morning before her grand party. Its stream-of-consciousness style and attention to detail reflect the narrative of *The Curious Incident of the Dog in the Night-time.*

- *Flowers for Algernon* (1959), by Daniel Keyes, is told through the viewpoint of Charlie, a mentally retarded adult who takes part in a science experiment and attains genius-level intellectual abilities only to lose them again.

Sources

"Asperger Syndrome Information Page," in *National Institute of Neurological Disorders and Stroke*, www.ninds.nih.gov/disorders/asperger/asperger.htm (July 17, 2006).

Gropman, Jackie, Review of *The Curious Incident of the Dog in the Night-time*, in *School Library Journal*, Vol. 49, No. 10, October 2003, pp. 207-208.

Gussow, Mel, "Novel's Sleuth Views Life From Unusual Perspective," in the *New York Times*, August 3, 2004, p. E1.

Haddon, Mark, *The Curious Incident of the Dog in the Night-time*, Vintage Contemporaries, 2004.

"Mark Haddon: Author Biography," www.randomhou-se.com/vintage/catalog/results_author.pperl?au-thorid=11481 (July 18, 2006).

Kirby, Barbara L., "What Is Asperger Syndrome?" in *Online Asperger Syndrome Information and Support*, www.aspergersyndrome.org (August 10, 2006).

Oakes, Keily, "The Curious Tale of Author Haddon," in *BBC News*, news.bbc.co.uk/2/hi/entertainment/3375965.stm (January 7, 2004).

"Poodle," in *American Kennel Club*, www.akc.org (August 10, 2006).

Review of The Curious Incident of the Dog in the Night-time, in *Publishers Weekly, April 07, 2003, p. 42*.

Review of *The Curious Incident of the Dog in the Night-time* (Audiobook) in *Library Journal*, January 15, 2004, p. 184.

Weich, Dave, "The Curiously Irresistible Literary Debut of Mark Haddon, "in *Powells.com*, March 28, 2006, p. 8.

Woolf, Virginia, *Mrs. Dalloway* Harcourt, 1925, pp. 3-5, 9, and 22.

Further Reading

Barrow, Judy and Sean Barrow, *There's a Boy in Here*, Future Horizons, 2002.

> A rare autobiographical account written by a boy with autism, this book provides insight into life with the disability.

Doyle, Sir Arthur Conan, *The Hound of the Baskervilles*, Berkley, 1987 reissue.

> This Sherlock Holmes mystery deals with a local supernatural legend about a seventeenth-century aristocrat and the violent family dog.

CPSIA information can be obtained
at www.ICGtesting.com
Printed in the USA
LVOW10s1001210118
563417LV00028B/233/P